TURKEYS!

A MY INCREDIBLE WORLD PICTURE BOOK

MY INCREDIBLE WORLD

Turkeys are large birds native only to North America.

Turkeys live in every US state
except Alaska (even Hawaii!).

There are about 7 million turkeys living in the wild, and over half a billion domesticated ones!

A group of turkeys is called
a **rafter** or a **flock**.

Adult female turkeys are called **hens**, and are about half the size of males.

Baby turkeys are known as **poults** or **chicks**.

Young male turkeys are called **jakes**, while young females are **jennies**.

Adult male turkeys are called **gobblers** or **toms**.

Male turkeys have a fleshy flap of skin that hangs over their beak, known as a **snood**.

They also have a **wattle**, which is a wrinkly and bumpy mass of skin under their chin.

Both the snood and wattle can change color based on the turkey's level of excitement or stress!

Male turkeys (and some females) have a tuft of feathers hanging from their chest, called a **beard**.

Only male turkeys gobble
(and it can be heard up to
a mile away)!

Females and males yelp,
cluck, and even purr!

Turkeys can fly for short distances.

They sleep (or roost) in trees to keep safe from predators at night!

Turkeys are **omnivores**, meaning they eat plants and meat.

They fill up on berries, grasses,
nuts, seeds, insects, frogs,
and even snakes!

Turkeys have strong legs,
and can run as fast as
25 miles per hour (40 kph)!

They also have excellent daytime vision, even better than humans!

Turkey feathers are **iridescent**, meaning their colors change when observed from different angles!

Turkeys are incredible!

Made in the USA
Las Vegas, NV
04 November 2024

11155968R00017